Life As ...

# Life As a Soldier in the Civil War

Kate Shoup

Cavendish
Square

New York

Published in 2016 by Cavendish Square Publishing, LLC
243 5th Avenue, Suite 136, New York, NY 10016

First Edition

Website: cavendishsq.com

This publication represents the opinions and views of the author based on his or her personal experience, knowledge, and research. The information in this book serves as a general guide only. The author and publisher have used their best efforts in preparing this book and disclaim liability rising directly or indirectly from the use and application of this book.

CPSIA Compliance Information: Batch #CW16CSQ

All websites were available and accurate when this book was sent to press.

Library of Congress Cataloging-in-Publication Data

Shoup, Kate, 1972-
Life as a soldier in the Civil War / Kate Shoup.
pages cm. — (Life as...)
Includes index.
ISBN 978-1-5026-1084-3 (hardcover) ISBN 978-1-5026-1083-6 (paperback) ISBN 978-1-5026-1085-0 (ebook)
1. United States. Army—Military life—History—19th century—Juvenile literature. 2. United States—History—Civil War, 1861-1865—Juvenile literature. 3. United States. Army—History—Civil War, 1861-1865—Juvenile literature. 4. Soldiers—United States—History—19th century—Juvenile literature. I. Title.
E607.S56 2016
973.7'4—dc23

2015023781

Editorial Director: David McNamara
Editor: Kristen Susienka
Copy Editor: Nathan Heidelberger
Art Director: Jeffrey Talbot
Designer: Joseph Macri
Senior Production Manager: Jennifer Ryder-Talbot
Production Editor: Renni Johnson
Photo Research: J8 Media

The photographs in this book are used by permission and through the courtesy of: J. F. Gibson/Hulton Archive/Getty Images, cover; American School/Peter Newark American Pictures/Bridgeman Images, 5; Brady National Photographic Art Gallery/National Archives, 6; Library of Congress, 9, 10, 12, 18, 20, 22, 24; BackyardProduction/iStockphoto.com, 14; MPI/Getty Images, 17; Karen Bleier/AFP/Getty Images, 21; Pangi/Shutterstock.com, 23; Omikron/Science Source/Getty Images, 27.

Printed in the United States of America

# Contents

# Introduction

The Civil War was an important war in United States history. Soldiers from the South fought soldiers from the North. It was the bloodiest war in American history. Many thousands of people died. Many were killed in battle. Even more died from disease.

At first, soldiers thought the war would be short. In the end, though, it lasted for four years. As the war dragged on, it became hard to find food. Many soldiers had little food to eat. Some had no shoes.

Eventually, the North won the war. If the South had won, our lives would be very different today.

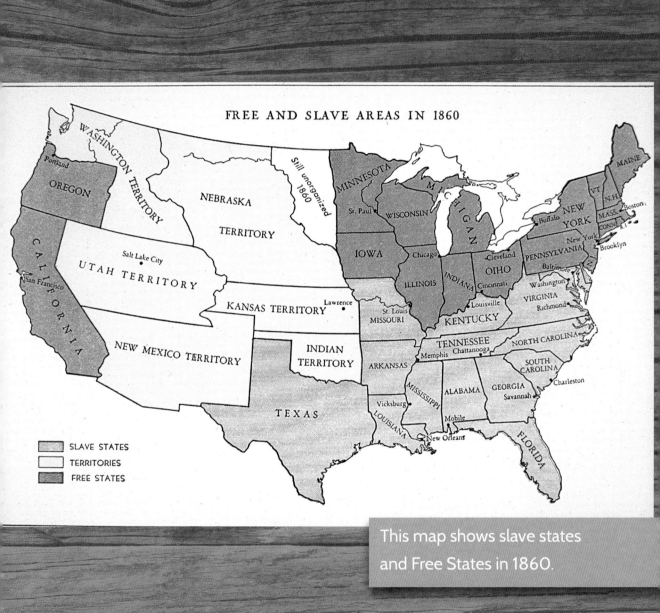

FREE AND SLAVE AREAS IN 1860

SLAVE STATES
TERRITORIES
FREE STATES

This map shows slave states and Free States in 1860.

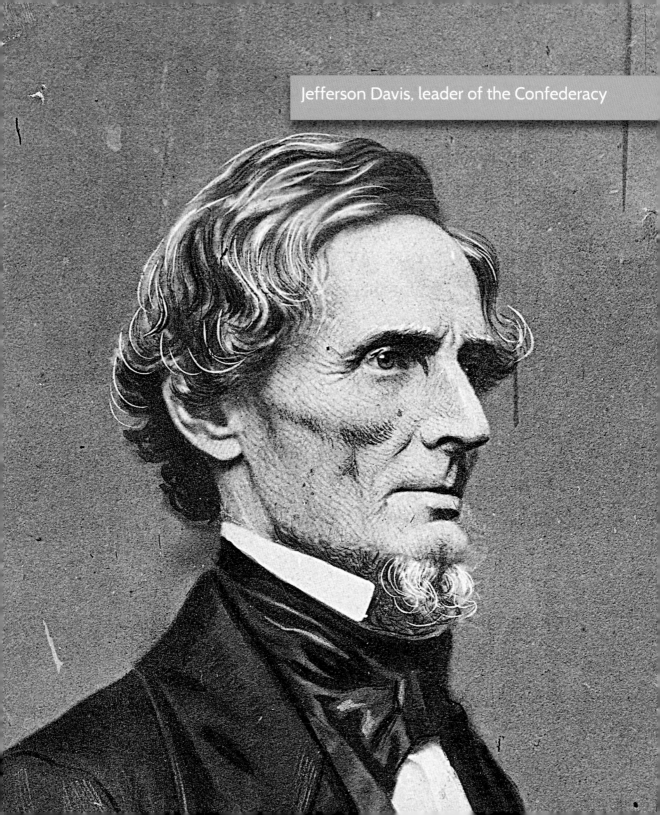

Jefferson Davis, leader of the Confederacy

# Chapter 1

# Setting the Scene

In 1861, many Americans who lived in the South owned **slaves**. President Abraham Lincoln, however, was an **abolitionist**. That meant he wanted to free the slaves. To prevent this, many Southern states split from the United States. This group of states was called the **Confederacy**, or the South. Its leader was Jefferson Davis. The states that sided with Lincoln were called the **Union**, or the North.

On April 12, 1861, Confederate soldiers attacked Fort Sumter in Charleston, South Carolina. It belonged to the United States government. The next day, Union soldiers inside the fort surrendered. This was the start of the Civil War.

The war lasted four years. Two famous generals were Ulysses S. Grant and Robert E. Lee. General Grant fought for the North and General Lee fought for the South. On April 9, 1865, General Grant forced General Lee to surrender. Soon, other Confederate generals also surrendered. The war was over. The North had won. The Confederacy was again part of the United States.

Over 2 million soldiers fought in the Civil War. 750,000 died. The Civil War was the deadliest war in American history.

## The Gettysburg Address

The Battle of Gettysburg was a famous battle in the Civil War. It was fought in 1863. It was won by the North. It was the turning point of the war. Four months after the battle, President Lincoln gave a famous speech at Gettysburg called the Gettysburg Address.

President Lincoln delivers the Gettysburg Address.

A group of men outside a Union army recruitment office

# Chapter 2

# Getting Involved

Before the war, the United States Army had 16,000 soldiers. After the war started, that number grew. In May 1861, both the North and the South wanted to get as many as 100,000 men to join their armies. By the end of the war, over 2 million men had served.

Some soldiers fought because of how they felt about slavery. Others fought to protect their homes and families. Some fought for adventure. Some fought because it paid them money every month. The lowest-ranked soldiers in the Union army, called **privates**, earned $13 per month (about $350 in 2015). Privates in the Confederate army earned $11 (about $300 in 2015). At first, soldiers joined the army

African-American soldiers during the Civil War

## African Americans

At first, African Americans were not allowed to fight in the Civil War. Even in the North, it was against the law for them to join the army. That changed in 1862 when Congress changed the law. Still, they earned less money than white soldiers.

because they wanted to. Later, both the North and the South forced men to join.

Nearly all Southern soldiers were born in America. Most soldiers for the North were also born in America. Some Union soldiers, however, were **immigrants**. Many were from Germany, some were from Ireland, and some were African American. Many of these African-American soldiers were freed slaves.

# Age of a Soldier

During the Civil War, most soldiers were between eighteen and twenty-nine years old. Men younger than eighteen and older than forty-five were not allowed to fight. Many lied about their age, however. The youngest Confederate soldier was Charles Hay. He joined at age eleven. William Black was the youngest to join in the North. He was nine years old.

The site of two major Civil War battles, the First Battle of Bull Run and the Second Battle of Bull Run, in Virginia

# Chapter 3
# Fighting the Civil War

There were many battles in the Civil War. Most were very short but very bloody. Many soldiers were hurt or killed in battle. Even more died from disease. This is because the camps where soldiers lived were very dirty. The most common diseases were typhoid and dysentery. Soldiers also caught measles, smallpox, malaria, and pneumonia.

Soldiers did not fight every day. Sometimes, weeks passed between battles. Every morning and afternoon, they did **drills**. Soldiers also did chores. They cleaned their weapons and mended their uniforms.

Union soldiers ate small meals of pork or salted beef. They also ate bread called hardtack. Confederate soldiers ate small amounts of bacon or beef with flour, cornmeal, or hard bread. As the war continued, meals got smaller. Many soldiers went hungry.

## Daily Schedule of a Soldier

**When they weren't fighting, a soldier's day might look like this:**

| | |
|---|---|
| Early morning | Wake up |
| Morning | Eat breakfast |
| Mid-morning | Complete drills |
| 12 p.m. | Eat lunch |
| Afternoon | Do chores and another drill |
| Evening | Eat dinner |
| 9 p.m. | Go to bed or do nighttime guard duty |

Confederate soldiers relax at camp.

Sometimes, life at camp was boring. To pass the time, soldiers played games, read books, and wrote letters. Sometimes they sang songs.

At times, soldiers had to move camp. Sometimes they took trains. More often they marched. Sometimes they marched 15 or 20 miles (24 to 32 kilometers) a day. They carried all their belongings on their backs.

Clara Barton, "Angel of the Battlefield"

# Women in the War

Women were not allowed to fight in the Civil War. Some pretended to be men so they could fight. One was Frances Clayton. She fought for the North. She was wounded two times—once at the Battle of Shiloh and once at the Battle of Stones River. More commonly, women served as nurses to care for the ill and wounded. One nurse was Clara Barton. Soldiers called her the "Angel of the Battlefield." Once, a bullet tore through the sleeve of her dress, but she was not hurt. Other women served as spies. Rose O'Neal Greenhow was a spy for the South. She used messengers dressed as farmers to send coded messages to Confederate generals. Harriet Tubman was a spy for the North. She also helped slaves escape the South on the Underground Railroad, a secret network of safe houses.

A member of the Union cavalry

# Chapter 4

# On the Job

Soldiers had many different roles in the army. Usually, soldiers were part of one section in the army. There were sections that fought on foot or on horses. Some Civil War soldiers served in the artillery, meaning they fought using large guns, such as cannons. Others served in the cavalry. These soldiers fought on horseback. Most Civil War soldiers served in the infantry, meaning they fought on foot. Some soldiers worked as doctors or cooks.

Just like soldiers could be in different parts of the army, they

A Union cannon

A Confederate soldier in uniform

also used different weapons. Soldiers used weapons such as muskets, rifles, shotguns, pistols, and even knives. Muskets, rifles, and shotguns are long guns that are usually fired from shoulder level. Sometimes, they have long knives called bayonets attached. Pistols are guns that are designed to be held in one hand. Most guns used in the Civil War shot special bullets called Minié balls.

In addition to their weapons, soldiers had other important items. These included tents, blankets, food, and bottles for their water, called canteens. Soldiers carried these items when they marched. Sometimes, their packs weighed as much as 60 pounds (27 kilograms).

A soldier's uniform was very important. It helped people tell soldiers apart and protected them in all kinds of weather. Union soldiers wore blue uniforms. Confederate soldiers had gray uniforms. As the years of fighting passed, these uniforms became torn and dirty. The soldiers' shoes wore out. Some men had to go barefoot. Other times, soldiers or shoemakers could mend the shoes.

Union soldiers wore blue, while Confederate soldiers wore gray.

## The Most Important Weapon

Rifles were very popular among Civil War soldiers. A rifle has grooves inside its barrel. These grooves cause the ball to spin, which increases the accuracy of the shot. One Confederate sniper, "Old Jack" Hinson, used a rifle to shoot Union soldiers. He was very accurate, often hitting targets more than a half-mile (0.8 km) away. It is believed that Hinson killed as many as one hundred Union soldiers.

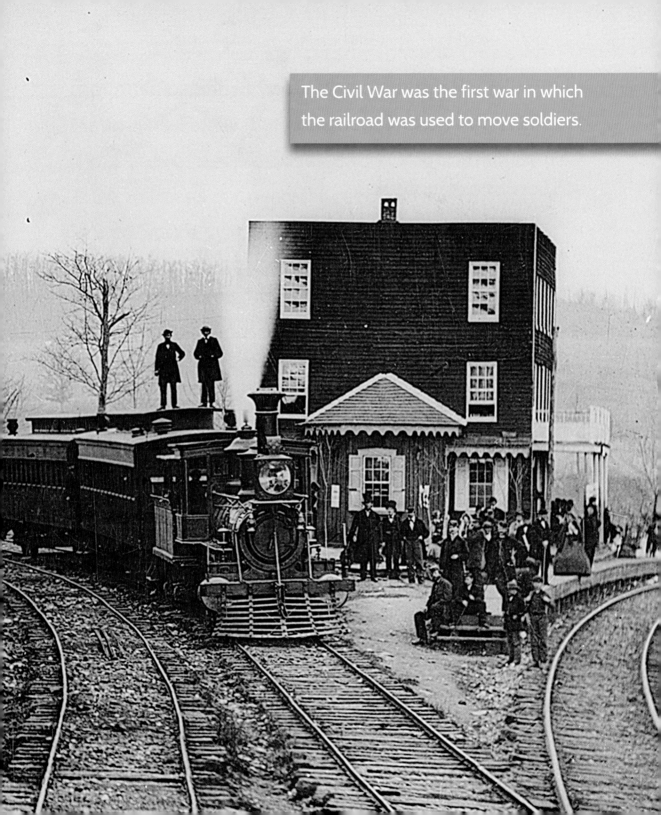

The Civil War was the first war in which the railroad was used to move soldiers.

# Chapter 5
# What the Civil War Means Today

The Civil War saw many changes to how wars were fought. It was the first time railroads were used to move soldiers. It was the first time soldiers used telegraph machines to send messages. For most soldiers, the Civil War was hard. Camp life was tough. Medicine was simple. Weapons were old-fashioned.

Soldiers on both sides fought bravely. The North had more men. This was one reason the Union won the war. Another reason was that the North had many strong leaders. Southern leaders like General Robert E. Lee were smart and tough, but they were no match for Northern leaders like General Ulysses S. Grant and General William Tecumseh Sherman.

If the South had won the Civil War, we might live in a very different world. America might be split into the United States of America and the Confederate States of America. Slavery might still exist. Many people prevented this from happening and helped America become the country it is today.

General Grant meets with General Lee
at the end of the Civil War.

# Glossary

**abolitionist** A person who worked to end slavery.

**Confederacy** A group of Southern states that split from the United States of America in 1860. Also called the South.

**drills** Exercises soldiers do to practice for battle.

**immigrants** People who are born in one country but move to another.

**privates** The lowest ranking soldiers in the Union and Confederate armies.

**slaves** People owned by another person.

**Union** The group of Northern states that remained part of the United States of America in 1860. Also called the North.

# Find Out More

## Books

Civil War Trust. *The Civil War Kids 150: Fifty Fun Things To Do, See, Make, and Find for the 150th Anniversary*. Guilford, CT: Globe Pequot Press, 2012.

Noble, Trinka Hakes. *The Last Brother: A Civil War Tale*. Ann Arbor, MI: Sleeping Bear Press, 2006.

Stanchak, John. *Eyewitness Civil War*. New York: DK Publishing, 2011.

## Website

**The Civil War for Kids**
www.civilwarkids.com

## Video

**The Civil War's Child Soldiers**
www.youtube.com/watch?v=Q52_MU4W_uE

# Index

Page numbers in **boldface** are illustrations. Entries in **boldface** are glossary terms.

# About the Author

**Kate Shoup** has written more than thirty books and has edited hundreds more. When not working, Kate loves to watch IndyCar racing, ski, read, and ride her motorcycle. She lives in Indianapolis with her husband, her daughter, and their dog. To learn more about Kate and her work, visit www.kateshoup.com.